Fantastic Fables

Hazel Morrow

authorHOUSE®

AuthorHouse™ UK
1663 Liberty Drive
Bloomington, IN 47403 USA
www.authorhouse.co.uk
Phone: 0800.197.4150

Published by AuthorHouse   02/05/2018

ISBN: 978-1-5462-8831-2 (sc)
ISBN: 978-1-5462-8830-5 (e)

Library of Congress Control Number: 2018901547

Print information available on the last page.

CONTENTS

FOREWORD

Although this collection began as a few poems written for my own children, it grew as the family did and now includes poems for young people of all ages, including the "young at heart" more mature friends I have had the pleasure of knowing over the years. The poems are probably at their best when read out loud and Jackie's illustrations have been left in black and white so that they can be coloured in (pencil crayons recommended, NOT felt tipped pens) if the reader wishes to do so. We hope you enjoy this book as much as Jackie and I have enjoyed writing and illustrating it!

DEDICATION

This book is dedicated to Roger, a very dear
husband and father, with thanks for his patience,
kindness and great sense of humour.

Hazel was born in 1949 and is a retired primary school teacher, specialising in teaching children with special needs. She is a Local Preacher with the Methodist Church in Macclesfield. She loves words, enjoys quizzes and puzzles and of course loves her family and friends!

Jackie is Hazel's daughter. She lives on the Wirral and works with primary school aged children. She enjoys various craftwork, being a Cub leader and singing with a local community choir.

ONE TUESDAY

One Tuesday we went down to the sea,

Just Rosie, my little black dog, and me.

Rosie galloped all over the sands,

I made a castle just using my hands.

The tide came creeping in silently,

Then galloped all over the prints of her paws,

The places she'd snuffled the sand with her nose.

It knocked down my castle, so no-one could see

A trace of Rosie, my black dog, or me.

ACCEPTANCE

The caterpillar starts his life as just a tiny grub.

Contentedly he'll chew his way through leaf and fruit and shrub.

He takes on all life offers him, and never questions why

He's been put here on this lovely earth, nor look up at the sky

To wonder who or what or where his creator might have been,

A caterpillar who reasons has never yet been seen!

Yet still he'll munch and crunch his food, and day by day he'll grow,

Until he finds he's "full to bursting" – faces a "Go slow".

Then sleep will come quite naturally, wrapped tight in his cocoon,

He'd never ask who gave him skills to spin, and yet, quite soon,

From sleep he'll come, new wings he'll shake,

No practice runs he'll need to make!

With hues of dazzling beauty he will flit between the flowers,

Not minding that his lifespan can be counted now in hours.

That little grub has reached, at last, all that he can be.

Lord, help us to learn acceptance, grant each one serenity.

We all go through different stages throughout our lives. The best thing is to accept each stage and make the most of it.

THE ADVENTURES OF HOLLY

Hello to you, my name is Holly,
I'm a black dog, rather small.
I'll tell you now of my adventures
That all started with a ball!

It was a lovely summer morning,
I was sitting in the sun.
Suddenly I heard a barking –
Millie from next door but one.

"Come and play with me" barked Millie,
"I have got a brand new ball".
Quickly I squeezed through the gateway
Hoping my master would not call.

I was just walking up to Millie's
When something moved. What was that?
In a flash I saw the culprit,
Next door's fat and grumpy cat!

Scraggy Aggy was this cat's name,

Chasing it was always fun.

Aggy took one long look at me

Then up she got, began to run,

All my thoughts of play forgotten,

Caring not about friend Millie,

Off I ran in chase of Aggy,

Little thinking I was silly!

Aggy dashed across the roadway,

I dashed after close behind.

Heard a squealing noise of car brakes,

An angry man's voice shouting "MIND!"

Up and down the streets ran Aggy,

Many roads and lanes we crossed.

Stopping, panting, I'd lost Aggy,

Then I knew that I was lost!

Looking all around I knew that
I had not been here before.
Now, beginning to get frightened,
Suddenly I heard a ROAR!

Looking up I saw a wagon,
Brightly painted red and blue.
On the side was yellow writing,
"White's Grand Circus From Belle Vue".

I had never seen a circus,
Pushed the red door with my nose.
In a cage were two huge creatures,
One stood, one tried hard to doze.

Never in my seven year life time
Had I seen any lions before.
They were so surprised to see me
They roared – I bolted for the door!

"What's all the fuss? A gruff voice bellowed.

In the doorway stood a man.

He caught me, grabbed me by the collar,

Dragged me to a caravan.

"Look at what I've found" he shouted,

As he bundled me inside.

Three small heads turned round towards me,

Six small eyes, surprised, grew wide.

"Has she got a name and collar?"

"Yes, but we could change all that.

We're leaving town tomorrow morning,

We need a dog. We'll call her Tat."

I was taken to a wagon,

Where they quickly locked the door.

There seemed no way to escape now,

So, tired, I lay down on the floor.

I felt the wagon moving slowly,
Then, at last, I went to sleep.
I was wakened up quite roughly,
"Come on, Tat, and earn your keep."

I was taken from the wagon
To the biggest tent I'd seen
I'd had no food and felt like crying,
They were being very mean!

I had a big white frilly collar
Fastened tightly round my neck.
They sat me on a stool and shouted
"Stay there!" I did feel such a wreck.

Then some music started playing,
And lights came on, so very bright.
Men in funny coloured costumes
Ran towards me, what a sight!

Suddenly I heard a voice cry,

"It's our Holly, Look, Dad, look!"

"I know that voice", I thought, and quickly

Jumped over the clown dressed like a cook.

What a noise! What a commotion!

Seats went flying, left and right.

People shouting, children screaming,

And so dark it was just like night.

"Holly, Holly, good girl, we're here",

Oh the joy of finding Chris

And his little sister Jackie,

Tail a wagging, licks to kiss.

I was taken safely home then

And given an enormous tea.

They had gone to the circus to cheer them up

As they thought they had seen the last of me!

Now it's another summer morning,

I'm back with my family once again.

Suddenly I hear Millie barking,

"Come and play out in the rain."

But by now I've learned my lesson

And think I'll be a sensible pet.

"You come down and play at my house"

No more adventures - - - not just yet!

THE COURAGE OF OUR CHILDREN

When we speak of wanting courage,

We may think of knights of old,

On trusty steeds, in armour bright,

All muscular and bold!

Then when we delve still deeper

Than those stories we've been told,

We consider those explorers

Who've defied the numbing cold

To be the very first to reach

Some God forsaken place,

Yet is it not as clear

As frozen nose on frozen face

That when courage is the chosen way

It cannot match the pace

Of the courage of our children

As they start this human race?

You can keep your book-bound heroes

For your damsels in distress.

And though I must admire those

Who face such great duress

Whilst trekking; sailing; climbing,

To be the first, the best,

Give me courage of our children,

As I'll settle for no less.

Sometimes things go wrong. We have accidents or become ill. It is then that we can learn a lot from the courage of our children, and keep soldiering on.

SAMMY AND CYRIL

Cyril the squirrel woke up one day
And thought "I need someone to come and play."
He hunted high and he hunted low,
He asked the rabbit, but rabbit said "No,
I'm much too busy to play with you,
You could go and ask the kangaroo."
Kangaroo was hopping round and round,
With his great big feet barely touching the ground.
"Oh no" he puffed, hardly stopping at all,
I just love jumping, I'm having a ball!"

So off Cyril went, still on his quest
To find a playmate, it's what he'd like best.
He came to a high fence and climbed up to see
At the other side, a big willow tree,
And there, sitting down in the tree's leafy shade
Was a little boy armed with bucket and spade.
Cyril leapt from the fence to the willow tree
And as he came down he could hear quite plainly
The boy was sitting there singing a song
That went like this "I don't know what is wrong,
I've played in the sandpit and run round the lawn,
But I'm tired of playing out here on my own.
I'd love a friend to play with me,
Then Mummy could ask him to stay for tea."

So Cyril thought "Maybe this is my chance

To make a new friend" and to catch the boy's glance

He jumped about on that willow tree,

He came down so far that the boy could see.

Then the little boy, who was Sammy by name,

Had a face that lit up at the thought of this game!

So for an hour they chased round the tree,

Playing "Catch me" and hiding till time for tea.

But when Mummy called Cyril wouldn't come in,

He jumped onto the fence and said with a grin,

"I'll come back tomorrow and play with you,

We'll play chasing and climbing and "Peek-a-boo".

And that night Cyril, curled up in his drey,

Thought of Sammy and all the fun of that day.

While Sammy was curled up in his bed,

With lovely thoughts inside his head.

Sammy and Cyril were friends for years,

They never fell out, and they shed no tears.

But Cyril was so nimble and free

No-one else ever saw him up there in the tree!

This poem was written for our first Grandchild, Sam, when he was a little boy. Was Cyril a real or imaginary friend? You decide!

REBEL

Some shattered glass, a broken chair
Why, Rebel, were you always there?
When there was trouble anywhere
Why, Rebel, were you always there?

A gate left open, with no care.
Why, Rebel, were you always there?
A cry of "NO! Well I despair!"
Why, Rebel, were you always there?

There, where you should never be,
Except when being called for tea!
THEN you'd be the first in line,
To gobble up your food so fine.

An angry neighbour shouting "STOP!

Or you will be soon for the chop!"

A dragging hand, a naughty dog,

Delivered home from smelly bog!

We HAD to take you back, you know.

Just couldn't keep, you had to go!

When there was trouble anywhere,

Why, Rebel, were you ALWAYS there?

Rebel was a very naughty dog who belonged to
my dear friend, Joyce Hackney. He was continually
escaping and causing havoc in the neighbourhood.

METAMORPHOSIS

I still remember, oh so well, when I was just a dot.

I'd lots to eat, a real treat, I couldn't move a lot.

All snug and warm and safe from harm, my life was a delight!

That's me in the picture - - - bottom row, third right.

Next there came the fateful day I wriggled myself free.

I'd scoffed so much, I felt quite butch, but still I felt like ME.

Darting around without a sound, we all had lots of fun.

That's me in the picture - - - my true life had begun.

I almost panicked when I found my tail had disappeared.

How could I swim? The thought was grim, but then I looked around.

New legs I saw, I thought "Oh corr!" and jumped out of my skin,

I landed on a lily pad and heard a dreadful din.

Without knowing why I did it I opened up my mouth.

I tried to shout, a croak came out, I found that I could sing!

The sun's so warm, I'm safe from harm, my life's still a delight.

That's me on the picture, singing with all my might.

Metamorphasis

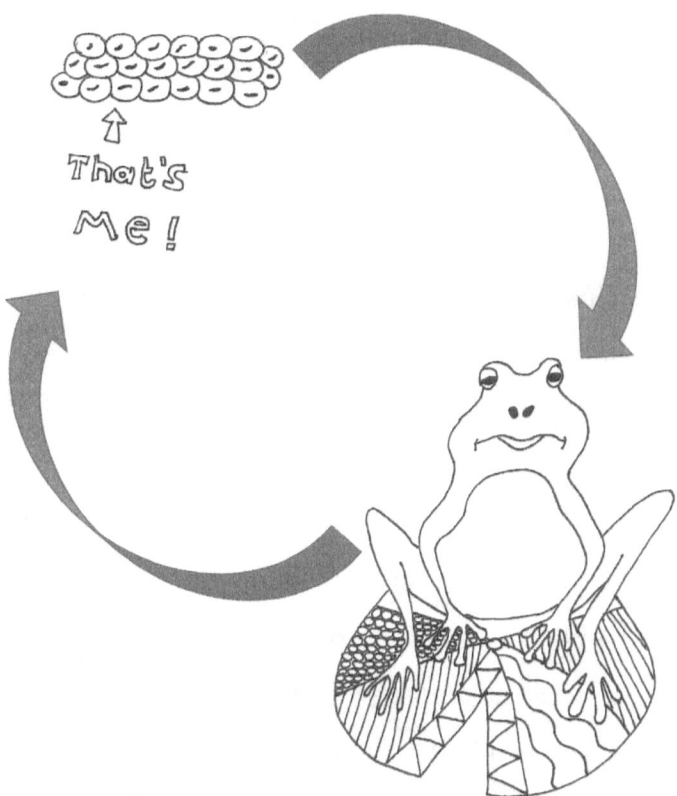

That's Me!

THE LAUGHING HYENA

Why does a hyena laugh so much?

Whatever amuses him so?

Why does a hyena laugh so much?

The answer I'd love to know!

We humans may laugh when we hear a good joke,

Or when watching a show we find funny.

We may giggle and wriggle when tickled on tum,

Till our sides ache and eyes go all runny!

Some people have laughs that are really strange.

They may bray like a donkey, alarming!

Their laughs are so highly infectious

They should carry a government warning!

Sometimes we laugh when we know we should not,

In the library reading good books.

We simply can't stop ourselves laughing,

Though we get such peculiar looks!

When it comes to the crunch we can laugh or can cry,

And I know which I'd rather do.

For if laughter is "The best medicine"

Then I'd much rather share it with you!

It is good to laugh, It makes us feel better, and as long as we laugh with other people rather than at them, it can do us a lot of good!

A TALE OF A TAIL

Why does a pig have a curly tail?
What use is that to a hog?
Does anything else have a curly tail?
A cow? A monkey? A dog?

A cow has a tail that flicks at flies
As it munches and crunches away.
It swings its' tail from side to side
Just to keep pesky pests at bay.

A monkey's tail is a wonderful thing
For holding on tight to the trees;
This tail is used quite magnificently
Letting monkey swing with ease.

A dog has a tail that is born to wag
When told that it's time for tea.
A dog's tail can talk if you listen hard,
It can say "come and play with me!"

So why does a pig have a curly tail?
If you know will you please tell ME?
But would we really want to know
And spoil one of life's mysteries?

CHARLEY'S CHIMP

One rainy Tuesday we thought we would have
a family outing to Chester Zoo.

So with Mum and Dad, Sam and me, Grandma
and Grandad and Erin came too.

We met in the carpark, weather clearing a bit, and set off to explore.

Located the toilets (most important), then
had choices and signposts galore.

"Where to first?" we excitedly asked, and decided to go see the apes.

So to Monkey House we made our way,
still in our raincoats and capes!

We saw the baboons, with their coloured
bums and gorillas galore, well a few!

Then we came to the chimpanzees where
they put on a show that was new.

We watched them for ages, transfixed to the
spot, as they swung around in the trees.

Their antics were marvellous to behold, they
performed with such skill and great ease!

Then glancing up to the corner I noticed another chimp.

He wasn't for joining in the fun and when walking he had a limp.

He was looking all sad and lonely, as if wondering what to do,

But I said "Let's ask the keepers why he is looking so blue".

We went inside to the kitchens, where the food was being prepared.

And there were two of the keepers, who looked like they really cared.

They listened while I told them of the chimp
with the limp who looked sad,

Then they came back round to the front with
us all, to see just what I meant,

Then looking concerned they got out their
radios and for the vet they sent.

The vet arrived quite promptly and went with them into the chimp.

He picked up one leg to see properly what
it was that was causing the limp.

So while the two keepers caused a distraction

With a pair of tweezers he made an extraction

Of a small piece of glass that the chimp had

Wedged up tightly in its foot pad!

Then he cleaned up the foot to stop infection

And gave the chimp a small injection.

He asked me what was my favourite colour and
I replied "purple, without a doubt"

He opened his bag and pulled right out a purple bandage, very nice!

Then he bandaged the chimp's foot up in a trice.

So the chimp with a limp walked up to his
friends and began once again to play.

Just then the sun came out, so we all had a lovely day!

We saw all the other animals too, but the chimpanzees were the best,

And the chimp with a limp made the day for
us and stood out above all the rest.

> The moral of this poem is Never be afraid to speak up
> if you see something that you think is wrong, but make
> sure you tell the best people to help you out.

ERIN'S ETERNAL QUESTIONS

If an elephant cannot pack its own trunk

How can it go away?

If an elephant cannot pack its own trunk

What chance of a holiday?

Poor old elephant must stay right there in the jungle!

If a kangaroo has no room in its pouch

For more than a joey or two,

If a kangaroo has no room in its pouch

What chance for a holiday roo?

Poor old kangaroo must stay by the Bungle Bungle!

If a big brown bear likes it not in the buff,

How can it leave its cave?

If a big brown bear has had enough

What chance of it having a rave?

Poor old bare bear must sleep the winter away!

If Erin cannot play out in the sun,

With her curly red hair and fair skin,

If Erin cannot play out in the sun,

How will she ever win?

Clever little Erin knows just what to do,

So a big hat and factor 30 means she will be okay!

Erin is five years old and full of questions! When it comes to advice about what you should do, always listen to your Mum and Dad, as they know best.

ARMCHAIR TRAVELLING

In my mind I know I can go
ANYWHERE in sun or snow.
I can travel around just taking a look
Without all the hassle of having to book.

Skiing gracefully over the snow
Without any danger of breaking my bones!
Travelling by trains with romantic names
Without constant beeping from mobile phones!

Lounging around on the beach or poolside
With no worry about the sun's harmful rays.
No clearing the sand from between my toes - - -
I could stay right here for days and days!

Just give me some brochures

And a guide book or two,

I'll be happy for hours with nothing to do

But sit in my chair daydreaming of you.

Just send me a postcard - - That shouldn't be hard,

And it really does show that you care.

I'll be with you in thought, doing just what I ought,

And not minding a bit I'm not there!

"Armchair Travelling" was written for my late mother in law, Blanche Morrow, who loved nothing better than getting out the maps and brochures to follow the journeys of her children and grandchildren.

ARMCHAIR ATHLETICS

In my mind I know I can be

The very best athlete you'll ever see.

Long jump, High jump, even the triple,

I can hear the applause start with a ripple

Then grow and grow till the stadium rings

To the cheers and claps my prowess brings!

Good medals galore will be pinned to my chest.

At running and javelin I'm simply the best.

I can leave all my rivals so far behind,

But as I'm not really the boastful kind

Maybe it's best to let others run free

While I stay in my chair watching THEM on T.V.

THE CAMEL WHO CAME TO TEA

I've often heard the camel called the meanest beast alive.

I thought it MUST be true, you see

Until this camel came to tea

And stayed from four till five.

He came to the door and hrrumphed and hrrumphed

And I thought he must feel quite ill.

But then very quietly he started to say,

In a very polite, slow and camelly way,

He had come to clear his name,

As he feared it was true

That me and that you

Thought all camels exactly the same!

Then he sat in the chair and he crossed his long legs

Where he shuffled whilst I made the tea.

So I put on a plate

What I thought camels ate,

Some sandwiches [with plenty of sand]

And a funny shaped biscuit or three.

So there we both sat with all sorts of things

Balancing on each knee.

I resisted the urge to ask "One hump or two?"

When putting his sugar in tea.

So still we both sat till, quite out of the blue,

He poured out this story to me.

"I was on my travels to holiday places, just taking a break as you do,

When I happened across this bounder in a bar near Timbuctoo.

He said that he was on the run and a master of disguise,

He boasted the police wouldn't catch him, as
they knew neither colour nor size.

He had dyed his own hair and he'd been on a diet,

Not stopped since Tunis where he'd caused a near riot'

Badly injured a lady so fair.

He'd left her lying there on the ground

With all sorts of people rushing around

And he'd scarpered without a care.

And I felt so bad, after meeting this cad,

That I had to come and find you

So please will you tell all the friends that you can

That it simply isn't true

That ALL camels are nasty and rude,

And are always in a bad mood?"

Then he uncrossed his legs, stood up and he bowed,

And he thanked me politely for tea.

So I'm writing for him, just to put matters straight,

And to say that I hope you can see

That in camels, like people, there's good and there's bad,

The same as in you and in me!

This poem was written for and is dedicated to Dr. Linda Craig.

THE POOR POORLY GIRAFFE

Why does a giraffe have such a long neck?

Whatever use could it be?

We all know the REAL reason,

For when eating from high on the tree.

BUT

Just think about it for some minutes

And let your thoughts run free

What could WE use a long neck for

If given to you or to me?

Imagine the view at a football match

When we go there to cheer on our team!

Or on the back row of the pantomime

Like the cat that got the cream!

We could laugh, we could shout

Till we're all shouted out and our throats become quite sore.

We could wrap up all warm

To keep us from harm.

We could wrap up all nice

on our mother's advice

Yet still we could end up

With hands round a hot cup

And feeling all shivery and cold.

We'd be put straight to bed

With "no arguments!" look.

Dosed up with medicine

Maybe given a good book

And told to "Stay there till you feel well,

Stay out of mischief and try not to yell!"

OH DEAR!!!

I can think of no creature I'd rather not be

Than a giraffe who has a sore throat.

The medicine you would have to take

Would be poured straight down your throat

You'd get no sympathy

For not fastening your coat!

Just think of a sore throat then times it by twenty.

You would have to sip soup and eat ice cream a plenty.

Yet was it all worth it, the cheering and shouting?

YES! If your team won, of that there's no doubting.

This poem was written for Susan Howell, a good friend who loves giraffes! The moral is simply that Mum knows best and you should always listen to good advice.

www.ingramcontent.com/pod-product-compliance
Lightning Source LLC
Chambersburg PA
CBHW030542290526
45786CB00004B/1830